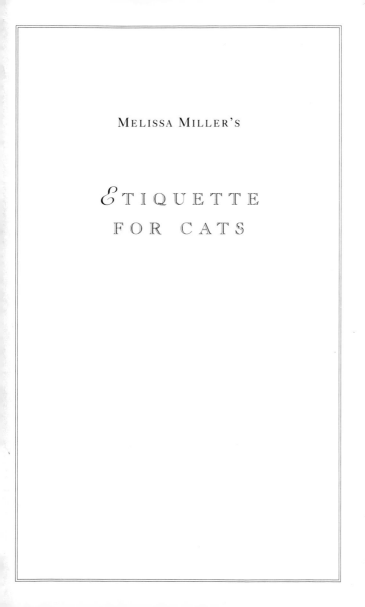

MELISSA MILLER'S

ℰTIQUETTE
FOR CATS

MELISSA MILLER'S

*E*TIQUETTE FOR CATS

Illustrations by Anna Currey

MICHAEL JOSEPH
LONDON

MICHAEL JOSEPH LTD

Published by the Penguin Group
27 Wrights Lane, London W8 5TZ
Viking Penguin Inc., 375 Hudson Street, New York, New York 10014,
USA
Penguin Books Australia Ltd, Ringwood, Victoria, Australia
Penguin Books Canada Ltd, 10 Alcorn Avenue, Toronto, Ontario, Canada
M4V 3B2
Penguin Books (NZ) Ltd, 182-190 Wairau Road, Auckland 10, New
Zealand

Penguin Books Ltd, Registered Offices: Harmondsworth, Middlesex,
England

First published in Great Britain 1995
Copyright © Melissa Miller 1995
Illustrations by Anna Currey

Typeset in Caslon
Printed in China by Imago

A CIP catalogue record for this book is available from the British Library

ISBN 0 7181 3922 4

*For my mother and her
country cat, Tammy Lee, who should
definitely read this book*

It's very hard to be polite if you're a cat.

- ANONYMOUS

CONTENTS

ACKNOWLEDGEMENTS

My sincere thanks to Anne Askwith at Michael Joseph for her careful editing and insightful thoughts on the structure and text of this book; to Julie Martin for her thoughtful designs; to Anna Currey for her wonderful illustrations; to Peter Carson at Penguin Books for believing in this idea; and to Abner Stein and Sandy Violette for their on-going support and assistance.

I would like to thank Maureen Day of *MIAOW!*, the Mensa Cat Group newsletter, who kindly allowed me to reprint several extracts from her readers' letters. I am also grateful to the readers of my own who have sent me their many wonderful and entertaining cat stories over the past few years.

For their permission to quote from copyright material, I would like to thank the following: HarperCollins Pubishers, Glasgow, for a quotation from the *Collins Concise English Dictionary*, edited by Patrick Hanks (first edition 1982); Aitken, Stone & Wylie for a quotation from *Jennie* by Paul Gallico (Copyright © Paul Gallico, 1950); *The Times* for an extract from their 5 March 1994 article, 'Feline Fable: even the death of a cat can make a moral for man' (Copyright © Times Newspapers Ltd, 1994).

Finally, my thanks to Julian Burney for helping me stay on course while juggling this book with my other various projects, and to Tiffy, my adorable little white cat, who has impeccable manners and was the inspiration for much of this book.

$\mathscr{A}$ MESSAGE FOR OWNERS

If you have picked up your cat's copy of this book, you might be thinking that 'etiquette for cats' is a misnomer – that the words 'etiquette' and 'cats' just do not go together. Most owners probably understand the word 'etiquette' to mean good manners, politeness, consideration of others and so on – terms which might not spring to mind when you are considering the behaviour of cats. Many owners are inclined to think of cats as too free-spirited and downright selfish to be called good-mannered in their sense of the word.

However, the word 'etiquette' actually has a slightly different and broader meaning. The 1989 *Collins Concise English Dictionary* defines the word 'etiquette' as the 'customs or rules governing behaviour regarded as correct in social life' or 'a conventional code of practice followed in certain groups'. In this sense, it is appropriate to apply the word to cats.

Cats can be loving, affectionate and, as sensitive creatures, considerate as well, capable of 'polite behaviour' – as owners would define it – such as using the litter box or rallying round when their owners aren't well.

But cats deem other standards of behaviour perfectly reasonable and correct too, such as walking off in disgust because Duck and Goose with Juicy Giblets now bores them, or refusing to act grateful for a stupid new cat toy or to display affection on demand.

Feline etiquette therefore differs from human etiquette in one very important way: it includes a wide range of often contradictory codes of conduct from which cats can pick and choose to suit the moment and themselves – unlike owners, who operate within a much more narrowly defined code of etiquette and often feel obliged to be polite whether they want to be or not.

The points of etiquette included in this book are simply a guide to the ways in which cats *generally* choose to behave in different situations. Owners should keep in mind that few of the points will apply to their cat all the time, and that the only steadfast rule which can be applied to etiquette for cats is that the standards can change – surprisingly quickly, very frequently and without notice – according to a cat's particular mood or motivation. Other than that, there is no such thing in cat etiquette as a hard and fast rule.

For the benefit of owners who read the rest of this book, the text is sprinkled with quotes and anecdotes from cat owners and cat lovers, which offer insight into and explanation of some of the finer points of feline behaviour and etiquette.

$\mathscr{I}$NTRODUCTION

Good manners and etiquette are extremely useful to know. Not only are they seen as a sign of good breeding; they also play an essential role in your quest to make life as enjoyable, comfortable and trouble-free as possible. This book is a general guide to feline etiquette and manners: it is full of tips on appropriate behaviour in a number of different areas, including situations which are particularly awkward or difficult to handle.

Of the topics covered, some of the most important are those involving owners, either directly or indirectly. Understanding as he or she may be, your owner will have certain limits which you should try not to exceed too often; it is therefore worthwhile to note those points which tend to matter more than others, listed for you in the 'Basic Etiquette' chapter on page 5. This leads us to the other most important point of etiquette – indeed the most critical to remember: *the importance of being charming*, covered on page 84.

The points of feline etiquette in this book are, of course, optional. The suggestions reflect the way you might behave in certain situations, not the way you necessarily *should* behave. A book on the way cats *should* behave would be entirely inappropriate: it is your responsibility as a cat – as well as your right – to define your own code of correct conduct. This will depend on your individual personality, your environment, and the type of owner that you have to put up with, all of which will influence your behaviour and therefore your manners.

I hope that this book assists you in establishing or even redefining the standards of etiquette that are right for you.

Good manners always means our own manners.

- G.K. CHESTERTON

NOTE: Wherever the text refers to the owner as 'he', 'his' or 'him', it should be taken to mean 'he or she', 'his or her' or 'him or her'.

$\mathcal{B}$ASIC
ETIQUETTE

Although most feline etiquette is essentially optional, this brief introductory chapter is meant to highlight those areas of etiquette which I feel are most important and strongly recommend for you.

None of the points listed below should be particularly difficult to adopt or adhere to, but by ensuring that none of them becomes a habit, you should be able to keep your owner sweet which, as you know, is actually in your best interest anyway.

TESTING YOUR OWNER'S PATIENCE

Amusing and fun as it might be for you to irritate your owner, he will no doubt have certain limits which you should acknowledge. Try to avoid doing any of the following on a regular basis:

- refusing to use your litter box, choosing the carpet or furniture instead;
- leaving your dead or half-alive prey around the house;

- meowing incessantly for no reason;
- waking your owner up for no reason.
- biting, scratching or otherwise harming your owner, for any reason;
- getting into the rubbish and strewing it around the house;
- ruining the drapes or other soft furnishings by scratching;
- tearing around the house noisily in the middle of the night.

You may well have other points which could be added to this list. Be aware of what most annoys your owner and how much you think you can get away with. Don't push those limits too often and when you do, be sure to follow up with a good dose of feline charm.

MAINTAINING YOUR ALLURE

Cats are usually very good at interpreting what their owner is feeling or trying to say. Owners tend to be extremely expressive and even when they do try to hide their feelings, their facial expression and body language often give them away. Cats can use this to their own benefit – it is useful to know what an owner is thinking, feeling or planning, in order to respond or react appropriately.

It has traditionally been more difficult, however, for owners to understand their cat. This is intentional on the cat's part and, indeed, one of the basic principles of the relationship between a cat and its owner.

The well-mannered cat will honour the reputation of felines as mysterious and captivating animals. While it is important to be able to communicate your thoughts and feelings effectively when you want to, it is imperative that you never let your feelings be known *all* the time; you then run the risk of losing your mystique, becoming transparent and even (perish the thought) boring.

Although to many of you maintaining your feline allure will come quite naturally, try to remember the following points:
- never be excessively chatty, emotional or overly dramatic;
- change your mind often;

- act completely dissatisfied often;
- keep the majority of your thoughts to yourself;
- never be too friendly to anyone you have just met;
- save your most meaningful meows, growls and hisses for moments of urgency or great importance to you.
- from time to time, sit still and stare straight ahead into space, as if you are contemplating a deep and meaningful subject (such as what you'd like for dinner).

Cats love one so much – more than they will allow. But they have so much wisdom they keep it to themselves.

- MARY E. WILKINS FREEMAN

$\mathcal{S}$OCIAL ETIQUETTE

The trouble with cats is that they've got no tact.
- P. G. WODEHOUSE

VISITORS AND HOUSEGUESTS

Guests and visitors to your home need not be greeted warmly . . .

. . . nor, indeed, at all.

You may wish to greet special guests, however, such as:

THE CAT-LOVER

THE GUEST WHO'S ALLERGIC TO CATS

and especially:

THE CAT-HATER

Cats always know whether people like or dislike them. They do not always care enough to do anything about it.

- WINIFRED CARRIERE

HOME ENTERTAINING

When your owner throws a party, it should be fun for you, too. Feel free to mingle with the guests if you're feeling very social, and plop yourself down in the *middle* of the room for your best chance of a back scratch or tummy rub.

If you're feeling territorial, lay claim to your favourite chair and strongly discourage anyone who is insensitive enough to try to move you.

Be sure to investigate any flower arrangements brought in for the party, to see if they meet your taste.

Parties are also an ideal time to sharpen your claws on the drapes or furniture, since your owner will probably be too busy to notice.

If food is being served, keep an eye out for guests who want a second helping . . .

. . . and, more importantly, those who don't.

Above all, don't forget – most good parties end up in the kitchen, so do your bit to help keep it clean.

Once the guests begin to leave, there is no need for you to bother to say goodbye, although it is fair to expect them to do so.

Whether you see the guests out or not, be sure to leave them something to remember you by. . .

NEIGHBOURS

The cat is a dilettante in fur.

- THEOPHILE GAUTIER

Neighbours can be a source of endless amusement. Not nearly as important to you as your owner, neighbours can be regularly terrorized or completely taken advantage of, as you please. You should use your best endeavours to reach your neighbour's house and introduce yourself, scaling fences if necessary. You can then assess whether your neighbours are 'Cat-friendly' or not, and consequently how to behave towards them.

CAT-FRIENDLY

If you are fortunate enough to have neighbours who like cats, simply turn on the charm for:

- supplements to your regular diet;
- alternative meals when your own doesn't interest you;
- a simple change of scene;
- the option of staying the night.

CAT-UNFRIENDLY

If your neighbours steadfastly refuse to admit how wonderful and rewarding cats can be, your only recourse is to pester them as much as possible for being that way. Suggested methods include:

- digging holes in their garden;
- using their garden as your litter box of choice;
- meowing loudly and continually under their bedroom window in the middle of the night;
- dropping dead rodents on their doorstep (or inside the house if you can);
- tearing up their rubbish bags when they're ready for collection;
- trampling through their flower beds;
- staring at them menacingly from a safe distance;
- fighting with any dog or cat that they may have as a pet;
- eating their pets' food;
- eating their food;
- making timely appearances when they entertain.

Bruce's favourite trick is to bring us back presents from other people's homes – I don't know whose. He has brought us a large blusher brush, a wedge of cotton wool, a fluffy toy and a Bonio dog biscuit. He seems to go for pink things more than anything else.

- JULIE KING

AWKWARD MOMENTS

From time to time, you may find yourself in certain social situations which make you feel ill at ease. Perhaps the company around you makes you nervous; you are caught off guard by someone or given a fright; you become jealous that another animal or person is getting the attention that you deserve; or you are simply feeling a bit left out.

In awkward moments such as these, the best thing to do is either run away and hide until things get better, or give yourself a bath on the spot.

Impromptu washing exudes confidence and a certain degree of apathy towards the situation at hand.

Whatever the situation, whatever difficulty you may be in, you can't go wrong if you wash . . . If you've started off to go somewhere and suddenly can't remember where it was you wanted to go, sit right down and begin brushing up a little . . . If you slip and fall off something and somebody laughs at you – wash . . . Remember, *every* cat respects another cat at her toilet. That's our first rule of social deportment, and you must also observe it.

- JENNIE, A STRAY LONDON TABBY
(as transcribed by Paul Gallico)

OTHER CATS

BEFRIENDING

Cats do not befriend just anybody. The cats that you do decide to become friends with, if any, should be selected very carefully and should of course be deemed worthy of your friendship. Usually, there is a special reason why you agree to accept another cat as a friend – he or she shares the same house as you or was adopted as a kitten and is like a younger sibling. He or she may live near by and be looking for a playmate, be always good for a gossip, or just be fun to be with. Whatever the reason, assuming the other cat also wants to be friends, it's better to go slowly and make a few, strong friendships than it is to have lots of shallow acquaintances.

Take your time.
Be choosy.

TERRITORY

Every cat has its own turf which is claimed as its own, and this should be guarded fiercely. Other cats, dogs and animals who unwittingly enter a cat's territory do so at their own peril.

Your territory will probably include not only the inside of your home but also any garden, patio or other out-door space that may be part of your owner's property. It need not stop there, however. If no claim has been made on the garden next door, you can incorporate that area as your own and should immediately inform the other cats in the neighbourhood accordingly. If you are the aggressive sort, you may be able to win extra turf by beating a defending cat in battle.

Never forget, however, that your own territory has to be defended, and you can employ almost any method necessary in doing so. No matter what type of personality you have, aggressive or docile, mean or kind, other cats are certain to try to encroach upon your own turf at some point in your life, and you must be prepared to defend it. Hissing, growling, arching your back and swatting are usually enough to keep an unwelcome cat on the prowl at bay, although some might need a bit more persuading . . .

I have been having a bit of bother with a neighbour, a cheeky cat by the name of Violet, who is very slim and agile, and sometimes jumps into my house through even the most inaccessible windows and makes straight for my food bowl. I take a dim view of this behaviour and so do my owners. They call her a witch cat because she [has] slanting eyes that give her a sort of evil look. I fear it may be some time before she learns the lesson that her presence in my house is not welcome.

- MINOU
(as transcribed by her owner, Vera Magne)

PROWLING

On many nights, especially if you are allowed outside by your owners, you may have the urge to go prowling. You might be in the mood for a playful fight, a good chat, a little romance, adventure, exploration, or some nocturnal hunting. Prowling is a multi-faceted activity at which felines are instinctively good, and prowling etiquette is equally straightforward:

never interfere with another cat's prowl, unless you are invited to do so.

ROMANCE

If you are lucky enough to get out and meet a cat that you quite fancy, you may wish to keep the following tips in mind:

- after a night of passion and romance, there is no need nor obligation to see your partner again unless you especially want to;
- males may have more than one partner on the same night and, indeed, it is considered quite macho to do so;
- females, however, are responsible for rearing any kittens they may have as a result.

DOGS

A dog, I have always said, is prose; a cat is a poem.

- JEAN BURDEN

Sometimes it is necessary to remind dogs that felines are superior beings.

Tiddles was taking a siesta stretched out on the front doorstep (as all geriatric cats are entitled to do). A neighbour walked by with her sturdy little Scottie dog, Muffin, [who] has the traditional antagonism to all felines . . . he pushed his nose through the gate and yapped furiously. Tiddles yawned and stretched then stalked deliberately to the gate and delivered a sharp one–two to the nose. The dog yelped and his owner immediately began to walk away, her precious animal trotting beside her . . .

Naturally, Tiddles felt this was too easy a victory and considered that a further warning should be given, so she squeezed through the bars of the gate and followed her victim as fast as her seventeen-year-old limbs would allow. Our neighbour put out her leg to protect the dog and got laddered tights and a scratched shin for her trouble. She [then] hurriedly dragged the dog into the safety of her own garden . . . We agreed to board up the gate between our garden and our neighbour's so that the animals cannot see each other . . . Muffin is now taken directly across the road before passing our house, but, just in case, Tiddles sits by the gate at 'walkie' time.

- BETTY HILL

BEFRIENDING DOGS

Although as a general rule befriending dogs is discouraged, you may meet a dog one day, or be forced to live with one, who is actually quite good fun. He may not be as smart as you are, and might have some peculiar habits, but he could become a strong ally, good playmate or companion. Remember, however, that:

- most dogs are inordinately friendly;
- it's almost always up to the cat to decide whether or not to befriend a dog;
- you can take as much time as you need before deciding to commit.

*All other dogs that you decide not to befriend should
simply be ignored.*

Daisy was a great trial to our dogs. Trixie the
spaniel was ten when she arrived and was incred-
ibly good and patient with her. Daisy treated her
as something between a second mother and a sort
of all-purpose plaything, swinging on her ears like
a trapeze act . . . But they liked each other – they
had a partnership whereby the cat killed birds
and the dog ate them, and when Trixie died Daisy
genuinely missed her and grieved.

- SALLY BRAY

GIFTS

GIVING OF

Gifts should be delivered to your owner personally, or left in a place where they won't be missed.

RECEIPT OF

Most cat toys are exceedingly dull and stupid. If you are given one, there is no need to feign either interest or gratitude.

NON-RECEIPT OF

Although it is most polite to wait until you are offered, if someone has failed to recognize that you'd really like to have something, you may steal it.

In a cat's eyes, all things belong to cats.

- ENGLISH PROVERB

$\mathscr{D}$ INING
ETIQUETTE

Never ask a hungry cat whether he loves you for yourself alone.

- Dr Louis J. Camuti

YOUR MEALS

No matter how often you are fed during the day, meals are sure to be one of the things you most look forward to. Most cats prefer to eat on their own, but even so a certain etiquette still applies.

It is impolite to put your food on the floor when a bowl has been provided. It's messy and inconsiderate and you then must rely on your owner to clean it up properly before your next meal.

Water and milk should be sipped lightly (to avoid dripping) and quietly (to maintain elegance) while dining.

Eat slowly. Never gobble down your food, slurp, grunt, cough or drool at meals. (Remember how unattractive this is when you see dogs eat.)

If you are fed at the same time as other cats or dogs, it is not necessary to wait for everyone to be served before eating.

Just because you have been fed, there is no need to thank your owner.

The same applies when given special treats.

A favourite meal, a handful of raw beef mince mixed with a few Go Cat biscuits, will earn a thank you, but any offering that doesn't measure up will get quite a different sound, followed by an unmistakable glare, and a resolute exit. He even knows how to make his cat-flap banging down behind him sound reproachful.

- TANIA PAYNE

If your offerings at mealtime are not up to scratch, it is perfectly acceptable to walk off in disgust . . .

. . . and to expect something better pretty quickly.

Silk (who is seventeen years old) only eats those tiny expensive tins of Gourmet and salmon Sheba – it's the only stuff she can get her teeth round now. The Gourmet is for her breakfast, the Sheba's for her supper. If I get it the wrong way round she leaves the lot. Still, at her age she's entitled to be a little eccentric and very spoilt!

- ALISON WHITING

If you know something better is in the cupboard or the fridge, it is wise to refuse your initial offering and wait for what you want.

At other times, you may not *feel* like having the particular brand or flavour you are given; in this case, you should send your food straight back to the kitchen – as often as necessary until you are satisfied with your meal.

The breeder had told me that [Raffles] was started on a cheap tinned brand 'so he won't get too spoiled'. What a good idea, I thought, naively; I'll go on with this. Raffles very quickly found it necessary to put me straight. It cost me a small fortune in tins, working steadily upwards from the very cheapest . . . (and eventually) settling for Whiskas – but only *certain* flavours, and these were and still are subject to sudden changes in personal taste, without warning. . . titbits are also expected from almost every meal or snack eaten in the house . . .

- TANIA PAYNE

OTHER PEOPLE'S MEALS

When your owner sits down to eat, remember:

punctuality is important.

If your owner is eating something that you particularly like, you may discreetly request a share.

If your owner has failed to recognize that you'd appreciate a bit of what he's having, you may find it necessary simply to help yourself (when the time is right, of course).

> **Bomb 'Abominable' loves to drink out of my glass by dipping his paw in and then licking it clean. He will do this until the glass is empty in most cases.**
>
> - RAYMOND TASH

Once we put some lamb chops (in a sealed bag) on a surface to defrost. We went out and when we returned, they were all over our flat half eaten. Scallywag really does live up to her name.

- DALE PREECE

However, no matter how tantalizing the food may be at your owner's table, under no circumstances should you ever – ever – beg.

ONLY DOGS BEG.

$\int$PORTING ETIQUETTE

It is axiomatic that you cannot order a cat to play. You can only coax and beguile.

- SIDNEY DENHAM

GAMES INVOLVING OTHERS

There is no need to play any game initiated by your owner unless you feel like it.

There is no need to play a game initiated by *anyone else* unless you feel like it.

What a piece of work is a cat! How elegant in motion, how fastidious in habit, how patronizing to the people it puts up with! Fond human bipeds imagine they own cats, and play infantile games of cat and pounce with their ungregarious lodgers, without realizing that it is their cats who are humouring them by playing games.

- *THE TIMES*, 5 MARCH 1994

If *you* feel like starting a game, you should expect your owner to recognize this immediately and to comply.

Once you are engaged in a game,
it is reasonable to expect your
owner to continue playing
until you are ready to quit.

However, *you* are free to call
it quits at any time.

THE GOLDEN RULE

You reserve the exclusive right to set the rules of any game you play, and to amend those rules to suit yourself – at any time, for any reason, and without any notice whatsoever.

Although all cat games have their rules and rituals, these vary with the individual player. The cat, of course, never breaks a rule. If it does not follow precedent, that simply means it has created a new rule and it is up to you to learn it quickly if you want the game to continue.

- SIDNEY DENHAM

GAMES OF YOUR OWN

CHASING THE IMAGINARY FOE

A simple but exhilarating game, this involves charging around the house for no reason, at great speed and usually in several different directions. Your 'foe' can take any size, shape or form that you fancy, or that your imagination can conjure up. At times, you may be chasing the foe; other times, it may be chasing you. This game is especially fun late at night when the rest of the household is trying to sleep.

CHASING REAL FOES: THE HUNT

Few things in life are more satisfying to cats than a successful hunt. It is to be hoped that you have the chance to go outdoors from time to time and, when the mood takes you, to look for possible prey. Hunting is a thrilling game, requiring all the stalking and survival skills you have inherited as instinct as well as techniques you may have developed on your own.

Should you come across another cat in the middle of a hunt, it is considered *extremely impolite* to interrupt or foil his attempt. It is best to spot prey of your own; and happily the range of cat prey is quite large. Whatever you catch should not be killed right away, but tormented and tossed around for a while. It should then be dragged back home half-alive, if possible, or simply abandoned once you're ready to move on.

> **Cats are not just pretty faces and fur. Claw and tooth, cats are the most efficient killing machines yet produced by evolution over millennia. They are the only creatures apart from humans to kill for fun, and to display a sense of humour.**
>
> - *THE TIMES*, 5 MARCH 1994

HIDE AND SEEK

As the name implies, this game involves finding new places to hide from your owner, then completely ignoring him when he tries in vain to find you. It can be played either outdoors or inside, and is a particular favourite among felines because owners hardly ever win.

TRASH THE CARPET

Offering the additional benefit of keeping your nails looking nice and trim, this game involves clawing the carpet with both front paws until tiny threads are extracted. Cats at an advanced level are able to create small holes. It is important, however, to choose an area of the carpet which is highly visible and likely to be noticed, so that your efforts can be fully appreciated by the rest of the family.

Variations of this game include Trash the Curtains, which can involve climbing and therefore much more exercise, and Trash the Upholstery, which is good for loosening up the back.

THE 'I'M STARVING' GAME
This involves pretending that you might die if you do not eat right away, then strutting off when you are fed.

THE 'I *MUST* GO OUT' GAME
Pretend there is some emergency and that you desperately *need* to go outside, then change your mind once your owner opens the door.

A cat . . . is always on the wrong side of the door.
- ALLEN AND IVY DODD

THE 'JUMP IN THE BOX' GAME

When presented with an empty box or container, no matter what its size, jump in immediately to claim it as your own. For those with a bit of imagination, it can serve as a fortress, a cat house or a bed. Once you've claimed the box, however, this game tends to lose its appeal until you are presented with a new box to conquer.

*Y*OUR
APPEARANCE

Cats are the ultimate narcissists. You can tell this because of all the time they spend on personal grooming.

- JAMES GORMAN

PERSONAL HYGIENE

There is no animal quite so fastidious about its personal hygiene as the cat. Its meticulous attention to toileting and maintaining a clean home base is one of the main reasons behind the cat's popularity.

- DR PETER NEVILLE, CAT PSYCHOLOGIST

Feel free to make a fuss if the litter box needs changing.

But do your bit to keep it smelling clean by covering up anything you leave there.

The earth-raking behaviour . . . continues until the cat is happy that the smell has reached the right level. This may mean total disguise, so as to avoid drawing attention to the depositor, or it may mean that the smell persists through the soil as a deliberate gesture to inform other cats of its presence.

- DR PETER NEVILLE

Tossing litter outside the box and strewing it around the house . . .

. . . is generally frowned upon.

> Gypsy hates to get her paws dirty, and so does her business on the patio and spends five minutes trying to cover it by scraping the cement.

> - SIAN BROWN

You may prefer a different area for your personal toilet (or be lucky enough to go outside). As long as it does not ruin any of your owner's furnishings or create undue mess for him to clean up, this too can be perfectly acceptable.

> Twiglet likes the idea of his own private facilities upstairs . . . He has noticed that water runs down the plughole in the bath. He has recently decided to add his own by sitting on the plughole and performing (only liquid I'm relieved to say). I think if my own toilet seat were smaller, I would be able to train him to use it.

> - ROSEMARY SUQQATE

Bad breath can be cured with a bit of parsley or a nibble of your favourite houseplant.

After a messy meal or a walk in the garden, it is advisable to wash up right away. It may be harder to do so later, you may be seen in this less than pristine condition, and, above all, you'll simply *feel* better.

> . . . there isn't an inch of herself or himself that a cat cannot reach to wash.
>
> - PAUL GALLICO

GROOMING

Be sure to bath at least once a day, more often if you wish.

It is perfectly acceptable to give yourself a full bath in public.

I have never seen a cat embarrassed.

- M. POINCARE

Hair can be left all over the house, because someone else will always pick it up.

To keep your coat looking clean and shiny, ask for a brush daily if you have long hair, and at least once a week if you have short hair.

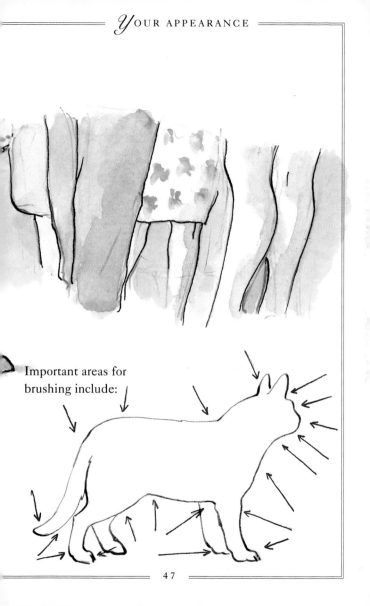

Important areas for
brushing include:

To keep your nails trim, regularly scratch any soft furnishings in the house or your scratching board, using both paws. Soft furnishings are good for polishing your nails, and the scratching board is good for filing them.

DRESS

As a cat, you are already perfectly dressed for all occasions. There are only two things you may have to think about:

BELLS AND COLLARS

Bells should be avoided at all costs, but if you are forced to wear one, you might try the following trick:

> **We bought Daisy collars with bells, but they weren't a howling success. Ever-resourceful, she'd swing the bell round to the back of her neck where it was silenced by her fur, thus enabling the pile of bones and feathers behind the dustbin to go on growing. Other times she lost the whole collar, once after only two days.**

- SALLY BRAY

Collars *can* be attractive, but most cats do not enjoy wearing them. If you have to wear a collar, hope for one that complements your colouring and good looks and reflects your personality.

Exoti-cat

Sophisti-cat

Bruiser

Classi-cat

Country-cat

YOUR FIGURE

Most cats keep a watchful eye on their figure. It is an important part of their overall appearance, and it affects the way they feel both physically and psychologically. If you could stand to lose a pound or two though, just remember this helpful tip from an American designer:

> *. . . overweight cats instinctively know the cardinal rule:*
> *when fat, arrange yourself in slim poses.*

YOUR VOICE

The way you speak will reflect your personality, looks and disposition. It is generally considered most attractive for cats to have soft and mellifluous voices which are not too scratchy.

But no matter how it sounds, your voice should be used sparingly to ensure it has the greatest possible impact when you do speak.

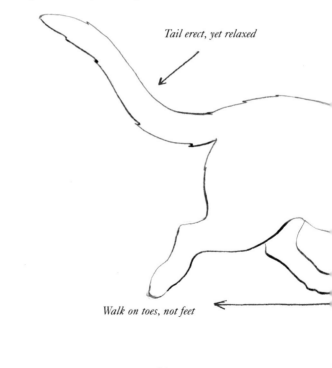

Tail erect, yet relaxed

Walk on toes, not feet

POISE AND POSTURE

Although to most cats this comes quite naturally, it is very important to have good poise and posture in order to give off the right airs of grace, elegance, superiority and finesse. To look, in a word, feline.

When walking, keep the following pointers in mind:

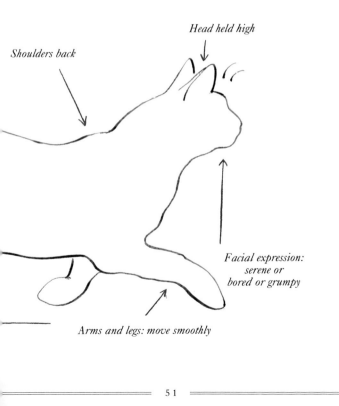

Head held high

Shoulders back

*Facial expression:
serene or
bored or grumpy*

Arms and legs: move smoothly

The tail, of course, must come forward until it reaches the front paw. Only an inexperienced kitten would let it dangle.

- LLOYD ALEXANDER

Other tips to ensure you look poised include:

never rush anywhere unless it is absolutely necessary.

Rushing can make you appear frightened and out of control, and is therefore an activity which is strongly discouraged (unless you are playing a game).

Strike graceful poses daily.

The importance of posing and looking statuesque cannot be overestimated. It contributes to your allure, which is a fundamental part of feline etiquette. In posing, keep your feet together, paws aligned, tail in, back straight, and remain quite still for an effective look that oozes self-confidence and superiority. Hold your poses for as long as you wish and try to strike them when someone can see you.

Poppy is . . . an extremely dainty tortoiseshell-and-white little lady. She always sits very neatly with her toes tucked in and her tail wrapped tightly round. When she walks or runs, she takes tiny mincing steps, as if she were balancing on high-heel stilettos. Her white bits are kept dazzlingly clean and there is never a whisker out of place.

- MARIAN CARTER

$\mathscr{D}$ IFFICULT OWNERS

Nobody who is not prepared to spoil cats will get from them the reward they are able to give to those who do spoil them.

- SIR COMPTON MACKENZIE

THE INSENSITIVE OWNER

The following are tell-tale signs of an insensitive owner, though this is by no means a definitive list – you may have other complaints that could also be included:

- sits in your favourite chair;
- ignores your requests for more food;
- doesn't realize when you want to go out;
- won't share bed;
- refuses to change litter box often enough;
- doesn't offer any snacks between meals;
- won't share any of his meals;
- turns on TV/stereo/all the lights when you're sleeping;
- is never affectionate;
- won't play games;

- won't clean food bowl properly before refilling it again;
- prefers dogs.

If any of these sound familiar to you, or are currently upsetting you, take note of these suggestions:

- make a bigger fuss when you are upset, to get the point across;
- adopt a different owner.

THE BOTHERSOME OWNER

Some owners just don't realize that their cats are independent creatures who, from time to time, must have their own space. Although they usually mean well, bothersome owners are overly affectionate and caring, to the point of becoming intrusive and annoying. They often can't resist picking up or stroking their cat, and rarely stop to consider whether the cat wishes to be stroked or not. When their cat complains, they usually misinterpret this as a request for more attention.

It should be said that some cats love this level of attention, but if you find your owner a bit onerous, the suggestions below may help you to cope:

- continually seek out new places to hide, which your owner is unlikely to think of;
- hiss, growl or meow more strongly when irritated;
- sleep in places that are difficult for your owner to reach;

- befriend a neighbour;
- spend as much time as possible outdoors.

THE ABSENTEE OWNER

Much as they may love you, some owners have certain lifestyles or commitments which require them to be away from home for long periods at a time. This can be extremely difficult on your relationship and requires a certain degree of patience and understanding on your part. It is to be hoped that there are other family members who stay at home more regularly to keep you company and look after you as required.

In the case of an absentee owner, there isn't much that you can do to rectify the situation, other than hope that the situation changes very soon. If your owner is so callous as to leave you absolutely alone for long periods of time, perhaps with a friend or other family member simply stopping by to feed you every day, then more serious problems are likely to develop. All you can do is:

hope for a change in fortune, or
seek a new home elsewhere.

THE MESSY OWNER

Humans are not always as fastidious and tidy as cats.

- Indoors, seek out places of your own which are inaccessible to your owner, and keep them as neat as you please.
- If irritated by a continually dirty litter box, hiss, growl or meow more strongly, or refuse to use it altogether, to get your message across.
- Spend as much time as possible outdoors.
- Befriend a tidier neighbour, as a retreat on particularly bad days.
- If all else fails, run away.

$\mathcal{U}$NAVOIDABLE
MISHAPS

Cats seldom make mistakes and they never make the same mistake twice.

- CARL VAN VECHTEN

ACCIDENTS

It is almost inevitable that you will do something one day which you did not mean to do. You may knock something over, break one of your owner's favourite or most valuable objects, or get underfoot and cause someone else to have an accident.

In such an instance, not only will you have to deal with the stress of the situation at hand, but you should also try to limit the damage to your image. It's important that you:

regain your composure instantly and pretend that nothing has happened.

FUR BALLS

An unpleasant but sadly unavoidable part of many cats' lives, especially for cats with long hair, fur balls do offer one tiny potential benefit. The next time one's on the way, try to cough it up in front of your owner. This may evoke a sympathetic response and perhaps a special treat.

CAUGHT MISBEHAVING

If you are doing something you know you shouldn't, and your owner catches you in the act, there are only two possible options. You can either:

take any punishment you're given,

or

run away and hide until your owner calms down.

Of the two options, most cats choose the second. Again, this depends entirely on your personality and the type of owner you have – whether he is easy-going or authoritarian, and so on.

HELPFUL HINT:
No matter what unavoidable mishaps occur, remember that they are just that – unavoidable. So, above all else,

never take the blame.

$\mathcal{U}$NFORESEEN CRISES

THE VET

Because going to the vet is such a traumatic experience, almost any type of behaviour there is acceptable. The following reactions are entirely suitable and can be given without fear of serious reprimand:

- crying;
- screaming;
- growling;
- meowing;
- non-stop meowing;
- hissing;
- bellowing;
- scratching;
- refusing to get out of the cat carrier;
- swatting at anyone who opens the cat carrier;
- clawing;
- biting;
- attacking the vet;
- attacking the assistants.

THE CAT CARRIER

The same type of behaviour applies, though to a lesser extent, to any trip in the cat carrier.

ADOPTION OF A KITTEN

This is another event in which you have no say and, almost certainly, no warning. The following tips might help you adjust to this unexpected and unpleasant addition to the household:

- bully the kitten into submission immediately;
- make sure it knows that you are the boss;
- insist on the same if not greater amount of attention from your owner;
- continue to sulk and act upset even after you've adjusted, for extra attention and special treatment.

Recently, I acquired Zack (a kitten). My older cat Boots had never had a cat companion. Ordinarily friendly and warm, Boots ignored me and sulked for about a week after I brought Zack home. A few days ago, I had to verbally scold Zack for naughty behaviour and Boots bit me on the ankle – not hard. I also accidentally stepped on Zack and when Boots heard Zack cry, he came running to see what happened. We've had Zack three weeks and now the two are inseparable.

- LAURA HESSE

ADOPTION OF A DOG

The same principles apply if your owner adopts a dog as those if he adopts a kitten. It is important to hold your ground, give nothing away until you are ready, refrain from being friendly until enough time has passed and ensure that *you* remain king or queen of the household (no matter what size the dog).

THE MEAN CHILD

If some of your owner's friends or relatives are insensitive enough to bring along their badly behaved child, or you come across one on your own, it is always best to:

flee and avoid the child at all costs.

MOVING HOUSE

Even for the most confident and adventurous of cats, moving house can be an upsetting and traumatic experience. Feeling unsettled, insecure and a bit frightened by your new, unfamiliar environment, you may pine to return to your old home, and may even try to do so if it's within walking or trekking distance.

If you are extremely unhappy in your new home, you are likely to crave much more attention from your owners; you may have trouble eating and digesting, even sleeping; you may also feel like hiding somewhere in the house for hours on end in order to 'blockout' the experience. In such a case, try to remember that moving is not the end of the world and follow these tips if you can:

- choose a small area of the new home to call your own;
- familiarize yourself with as much of the indoor space as you can, and watch your confidence grow as you do so;
- don't overeat or change your regular dining habits;
- ask for as much extra attention and reassurance from your owner as you need.

> . . . once at the new house . . . the tricks of short frequent feeds and plenty of love and attention against a secure background should help [your cat] build new bonds. The new home should come to be perceived as the centre of the new territory and a source of food and shelter.
>
> - DR PETER NEVILLE

THE BATH

Baths can be terrifying experiences. They incorporate many of the things you probably hate the most – not being in control of a situation, being 'forced' to do something that wasn't your own idea, getting soaking wet and being scrubbed with a repulsive substance that smells nothing like French perfume. What's more, baths are almost always a completely redundant exercise for everyone involved since you already give yourself at least one bath a day.

Nevertheless, many owners insist upon them, and when it's suddenly your turn, there is little you can do to stop it.

Although baths tend to finish sooner if you tough them out and remain still, the following reactions are also acceptable and may discourage your owner from giving you *quite* so many:

- screaming,
- growling,
- crying,
- moaning,
- biting,
- scrambling,
- kicking,
- clawing,
- scratching,
- splashing,
- fidgeting,
- fidgeting wildly, and
- any combination of the above.

After a bath, you may wish to:

- mope,
- sulk,
- vigorously shake yourself dry (spraying owner),
- drip water all over the carpet and upholstered furniture, and
- hide.

$\mathcal{D}$OMESTIC ETIQUETTE

The majority of cat people, deep down, have a sneaking and half-recognized suspicion that they have been taken over by their feline, four-footed friend and that to a considerable extent she has imposed her whims and wishes upon the household.

- PAUL GALLICO

GREETING YOUR OWNER

LAZY METHOD

ENERGETIC METHOD

- Wind around both his legs.
- Chase his feet or ankles.
- Continually position yourself where his next step would naturally be.

RESPONDING TO YOUR OWNER

HOW TO RESPOND WHEN YOUR NAME IS CALLED

HOW TO RESPOND TO A COMMAND

A cat is there when you call her – if she doesn't have something better to do.

- BILL ADLER

HOW TO RESPOND TO WHEN YOUR OWNER OFFERS TO PLAY

HOW TO RESPOND WHEN CALLED IN FOR DINNER

CHOOSING YOUR MOMENT

Certain times are better than others to ask for attention or anything else from your owner. The best are when it inconveniences him to comply.

Particularly good moments include any time that your owner is engaged in one of the following activities:

- reading,
- napping,
- sleeping,
- entertaining,
- working,
- talking on the phone, or
- exercising.

HOUSEPLANTS

Although probably not purchased with you in mind, houseplants can be nibbled on as a tasty snack and are also a wonderful source of extra vitamins and nutrients. They are especially useful to cats who are not allowed outdoors. You should be able to tell instinctively which plants are edible and which plants to stay away from. Just take care that your owner doesn't catch you nibbling away at his houseplants too often.

> **Most cats eat more plant material than we realize, probably in an effort to obtain a quickly digestible source of vitamins and minerals and roughage. Some regurgitate the grass with a portion of their dinner and this is believed to be a natural method of worming or helping to eject hairballs . . . Indoor cats should be provided with a tub of seedling sprouts to munch on, so as to discourage consumption of houseplants.**
>
> - DR PETER NEVILLE

SMALL MISUNDERSTANDINGS

Effective communication between you and your owner is vital to the success of your relationship and, more importantly, your happiness. When you want to do so, you must be able to convey to your owner exactly how you are feeling. In many cases, you need not utter a single sound but can use your eyes and facial expression to get your point across. For example:

'Hey – you're sitting in my chair.
Please get out, now.'

'Yes, I'm in your chair. So?'

'Can't you see I'm trying *to get some sleep?'*

'You know I can't stand this flavour.
Please give me something which doesn't
taste/look/smell so horrible.'

SLEEPING
ARRANGEMENTS

There are people who reshape the world by force or argument, but the cat just lies there, dozing, and the world quietly reshapes itself to suit his comfort and convenience.

- ALLEN AND IVY DODD

WHERE TO SLEEP

DAY
- In the sun.
- In the shade.
- In the middle of the floor in the busiest room of the house.
- In your owner's favourite chair.
- In your favourite chair (if different from above).
- Near a window.
- In the garden
- On the patio.
- On the roof.
- In the cupboard full of jumpers.
- In a drawer.
- On a table.

- On a bed.
- On the sofa.
- On a pillow.
- On a rug.
- Underneath large pieces of furniture.
- On top of a large piece of furniture.
- In someone's lap.
- In a box.
- Any place that's warm.

NIGHT

- On or in your owner's bed (width-wise).
- Anywhere on top of your owner.

HELPFUL HINT:

When lounging or sleeping on a sofa or bed, there is no need to limit yourself to just one place when you could take up two.

Baldrick enjoys sharing my bed. This would be OK if the bed was twice the size it is (it's a double). He seems to fill it and I wake up practically falling out.

- MADDY WILKS

WHEN TO SLEEP

Any hour of the day or night (for as long as you please).

A little drowsing cat is an image of perfect beatitude.

- CHAMPFLEURY

DISTURBANCES

Sadly, most people and other animals do not understand how important sleep is to cats. Presumably
because cats need so much sleep (eighteen hours on
average), and because they do most of their sleeping
during the day, owners tend to regard it as excessive,
unnecessary or even a sign of their cat's laziness.
Whether or not such conclusions are true is not for cats
to waste time considering; the more immediate problem is the constant barrage of interruptions that almost
all cats suffer daily in their quest to get in those crucial
hours of beauty sleep – the doorbell, the hoover, the
screaming child, the dog, the telephone . . . the list
goes on and on.

There is no need for you to have to cut back on the
number of hours you sleep, or to suffer unnecessary
interruptions. Simply avoid the problem altogether by
sleeping in rooms or areas of the house where you
know you will be left alone, and where it is usually
quiet. Alternatively, you may prefer to nap outdoors if
you can, somewhere hidden, inaccessible and private.

Disturbances are a different matter altogether, though,
when it comes to your *owner's* sleeping time . . .

WAKING UP YOUR OWNER

Owners don't need nearly as much sleep as cats, and you should therefore have no qualms about interrupting them as they snooze. There are literally hundreds of possible reasons why you may feel it necessary to wake your owner up, although having a good reason to is not a prerequisite. The most common excuses are:

- you're hungry;
- you're thirsty;
- you're bored;
- you want to go out;
- you want him to open the front door, but you don't want to go out;
- you want him to open the back door, but you don't want to go out;
- you want to sleep exactly where he's sleeping;
- you want him to stop snoring;

- you want to play;
- you want some attention;
- you just feel like it.

Just as there are numerous reasons why you may need to wake your owner, there are also many different ways of actually waking him up. Suggested methods include:

- loud and continual meowing;
- joining him or her in bed and changing your position every two minutes;
- sharpening your claws on his body;
- sitting near his head and purring very loudly;
- walking repeatedly over his chest or abdomen.

It is impossible to oversleep in our house as both Bella and Barney wake us up before the alarm by rattling the blinds then walking all over us.

- MRS J. MACMASTER

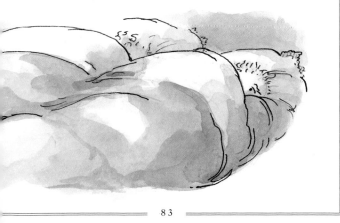

𝒯HE IMPORTANCE
OF CHARM

Cat owners are usually willing to put up with much more from their pet than owners of other animals. However, they will almost certainly take a much kinder view of their cat if they receive a bit of affection from you every now and then.

Ingratiate yourself with your owner in any way you please – a sweet meow and batted eyes; a full and happy purr; or a snuggle in his lap. Condescend to play those silly little games with him sometimes when asked. What you choose to do depends on your personality and what you feel comfortable with, as well as the response you get from your owner.

You shouldn't be *overly* charming, lest your owner comes to expect such attention, or worse, begins to take you for granted. But such 'good' behaviour can often excuse some of your other antics that are considered less appealing.

The relationship between cats and owners is still something of a trade-off. In exchange for a regular food supply, warm shelter, general care and almost free run of their owner's home, cats grace the home with their presence and provide their owners with just enough – but not too much – charm, love and entertainment value to keep them very happy.

The importance of being charming is probably the most important point of this book to remember. Otherwise, your feline etiquette might be too much for your owner to bear!

> I live with two cats . . . I can't pretend that they live with me because they run the house and everything revolves around them . . . Where do I fit into the scheme of things? Well, like most cats' lodgers, I'm there to mop up on the odd occasion when there is an accident; I provide the transport and fees for the vet when sickness rears its ugly head; I am a feeding machine, a door opener, a ward and comfortable cushion, and something to lash out at when tempers flare . . .
>
> Even in my menial position in the household, I adore these animals who can also be so soft and loving, and I know that without them my life would be much the poorer and exceedingly dull.
>
> - SHEILA FOWLER